GLUTEN-FREE WEIGHT TRAINING DIET

Make each meal an opportunity to improve your body

Mariana Correa

Certified Sports Nutritionist

Copyright Page

2014 Gluten-free Weight Training Diet

ISBN 1511985054

Acknowledgement

To my coach, thank you for teaching me that with hard work and dedication anything is possible. your love and support has helped me become everything I am today.

I will be forever grateful.

About the author

Mariana Correa is a certified sports nutritionist and former professional tennis player.
Mariana reached a career high of 26 in the world in juniors with wins over Anna Ivanovich (former #1 WTA in the world) and many other top 100 WTA players.

She competed successfully all over the world in over 26 countries and hundreds of cities including in London for Wimbledon, Paris for the French Open and in Australia for the world championships. She also represented Ecuador in Fed Cup, where the team reached the finals in their group.

During her career she was awarded the fair play award many times, proving to be not only an excellent player, but also a role model for other athletes.

Being an athlete herself she understands what it takes to be the best in what you love.

Mariana is a certified sports nutritionist with years of experience in proper nutrition and hydration for high performance athletes.

She combines her love and knowledge in sports and nutrition in this book to provide you with all the information you need to succeed.

Description

Gluten-free Weight Training Diet is the best book for anyone who is looking to be stronger, faster and fitter when performing. The only way to achieve this is if your body is healthy from the inside out. Allow your body to perform at it maximum potential.

Your connection with food is the biggest influence for your long-term well-being. The first thing to consider when you would like to make a change in your life is your diet. Nutrition is the foundation of your lifestyle and athletic development.

You will improve your performance through nutrition. This book includes a clear explanation of what you need to succeed and includes over 50 recipes that will set you on the path of greatness.

The author Mariana Correa is a former professional athlete and certified sports nutritionist that competed successfully all over the world. She shares years of experience both as an athlete and a coach bringing a priceless perspective.

A year from now you will be wishing you had started today. The journey to greatness is not easy, but every step you take forward brings you one step closer to your goals.

Get started today you will be on your way to be healthier, fitter and happier.

Table of Contents

Table of Contents

Introduction

Achieve your Objectives

"Most people have no idea how amazing their body is designed to perform" Mariana Correa

Let's begin by understanding your body is perfection. Yes, no matter what you think it's perfect. Every single cell works together in synchronicity allowing you to be healthy and perform your everyday activities and training.

Do you have any idea of all the cells that are working together in order for you to read this book or something as simple as the process of breathing? Your body is incredible, but in order to stay in top shape it needs your help.

An active lifestyle combined with good nutrition is the best way to stay healthy.

But in this book we'll take it a notch further, we not only want to be healthy we want to be at the top of our game. Take that perfect body to the next level, the ultimate level.

We will go through several steps in this book to learn how to turn your body into the ultimate performance machine.

The word Diet comes from the Greek language and means "way of life." Therefore we should represent healthy eating and dieting as a **'lifestyle'** not a set of rules set in stone we need to follow.

Nutrition is eighty percent habit. You most likely have had the same nutritional habits for years and years. It will take time, discipline and constant support to change your habits and reach your potential.

If you've been eating toaster waffles with maple syrup for breakfast since you were a kid it won't be easy to change that now after all these years. You might think you're fine and no harm has come from this. Wrong! The hydrogenated fat in the frozen waffle and the high fructose corn syrup in your maple syrup are definitely not helping you to achieve your potential.

In our current time sports are becoming even more demanding than ever. Athletes need to be stronger, fitter and faster. And a good training program by itself won't even get you midway to the body you need to be the best.

Yes, it's absolutely necessary to have a great training program and without it you won't accomplish much, but any champion can tell you that the single most important factor in creating the ultimate body is a proper nutrition plan.

There is only enough room at the top for the ones who really want it.

Nothing will ever come for free or granted. Do you love it enough to fight day in and out to reach your goals?

Yes! Wonderful, then let's get started.

Chapter 1

Gluten Freedom

"I eat gluten-free because it allows me to train harder and achieve better results." M. Correa

The gluten-free diet is a focus on eating natural, real food that is available in nature all around us with little or no processing. The gluten-free diet focuses on avoiding the protein gluten.

Surprisingly our bodies are not well suited to eat what we tend to eat these days. From large amounts of sugar to processed grains, these foods are definitely not helping us achieve our potential.

Gluten is made primarily of two protein groups gliadin and glutenin that combine together when flour and water are mixed to make dough for bread or another processed food. Mixed they provide structure and elasticity in the dough for bread, pizza, baked goods and other processed foods.

Gluten is found in wheat and in other grains such as barley and rye. It would be easy to simply avoid bread, pasta and cakes with gluten but gluten is now present in soups, snack foods, sauces, cereals, sweets, and a wide range of other products.

Wheat is easy to grow, to stock and to distribute. The properties of flour and dough make wheat adaptable and easy to use. Many athletes don't realize that many foods they normally consume contain gluten. In America nearly a third of the foods found in the supermarket contain some component of wheat which is usually gluten or starch and sometimes both.

More than half of the items in the supermarket are processed foods that last for years in a can, or pasta boxes that last months before expiring. Snacks full of all sorts of strange ingredients, many even unpronounceable.

Celiac Disease

The main reason for many to switch to a gluten-free diet is because they have celiac disease. Now research has proven that many have the same negative symptoms to gluten even without celiac disease, these individuals are referred to as non-gluten sensitive. Celiac disease is an immune disease in which individuals cannot consume gluten because it damages their small intestine.

Many times the symptoms appear right after a meal and fade quickly. In other cases the symptoms can last for days or chronically which can lead to the diagnosis of an autoimmune disease instead of gluten sensitivity.

Gluten can affect each individual differently, but some of the most common symptoms are:

- Irritability
- Digestive Problems
- Bloating
- Sluggishness
- Abdominal cramping
- Diarrhea
- Headaches
- Lack of balance
- Dizziness
- Chronically fatigued
- Brain fogged
- Inflammation in the joints
- Low immunity (constantly sick)

As you can see absolutely none of these symptoms will help you perform better. Quite the contrary, a normal individual can barely function properly with these symptoms, there is no way an athlete could ever perform his best this way.

Many athletes are now adapting their lifestyle to gluten-free and enjoying the benefits from this change. The best example is Novak Djokovic, a professional tennis player who did not know he had celiac disease, he suffered from exhaustion, digestive problems, lack of balance and many other symptoms. As soon as he discovered he had celiac disease he made the change to gluten-free and saw incredible results. He won the first 41 matches he played and finished the year with a record 70-6 winning 3 grand slams. Djokovic says this change was essential to achieve his accomplishment.

There has been much debate nowadays to whether gluten sensitivity is a real condition or it's simply a condition created by picky eaters. There is a test that can prove is you have celiac disease, but then again this test cannot demonstrate whether you are non-gluten sensitive. It's estimated that 99% of the individuals who have celiac disease or are sensitive to gluten are never diagnosed.

The best way to find out if you are sensitive to gluten would be to first list every single symptom that bothers you, even if it's chronic or sporadic. List all of them, don't try to explain them away, like my back problems are from sitting too much.

Second go on a complete gluten-free diet for 60 full days. Gluten is a very large protein and takes months to clear out from your system. If you can't do this chances are you're addicted to gluten as we are often addicted to things were allergic to.

After the first 60 days of being gluten-free review your list and notice how many of these symptoms still remain. If the symptoms have disappeared you will definitely want to continue this route. If you're not sure whether these changes have made a difference go back to your former diet and see if those symptoms come back stronger than before.

How to handle Gluten Intolerance?

There is no shortcut to being healthy and at the top of your game. There is only way to be the best you can by eliminating gluten 100% of your diet, even the smallest trace of gluten can set you back.

Many individuals try different approaches such as taking a cheat day or the weekend off from the diet, but this will not work. As we have read above gluten remains in your system for months sometimes.

Switching to a gluten-free diet is a big adjustment and like anything new, it will take some getting used to. At the beginning you might feel deprived by the restrictions from the diet, but it helps to focus on all the foods you can eat instead.

You will be pleasantly surprised at how many products are now gluten-free, such as bread, pasta and even pizza.

With so many individuals realizing they are sensitive to gluten big companies are making their products available gluten-free. From big cereal companies to pizza makers such as Pizza Hut they have finally acknowledged the need for gluten-free products and more products will continue to become available so stay positive and don't give in to gluten.

Many studies have demonstrated that an astounding amount of diseases and lifestyle issues can be reversed with these simple changes in your diet.

Stay Positive, you will feel healthier, have more energy, and perform your best. You will most likely lose some pounds of fat as well. No top athlete needs to carry around excess pounds of fat, so this is a very good thing.

Chapter 2

Gluten-Free Meals

"You don't have to be great to start, but you have to start to be great." Zig Ziglar

Are you wondering which foods contain gluten and which don't? The gluten free diet can be tricky and gluten can sneak into some very unexpected places. If you're just getting started with this diet it's understandable to get confused with ingredients and labels. This book will help guide you into foods that are not allowed and the many healthy options you have available.

Cutting out gluten from your diet might seem like a difficult and limiting mission. You might be thinking about your favorite pizza or your delicious chocolate cake, but fortunately there are many alternative ingredients that can still make your favorite recipes possible with great flavor as well as gluten-free.

Try to stay focused on all the delicious foods available as gluten-free and think about all the great improvements your body will do.

Let's review the main 6 food groups you need to concentrate on to stay in a naturally gluten-free path:

- Fruits
- Vegetables
- Meats and Poultry
- Fish and Seafood
- Dairy
- Beans, nuts and legumes

Organic Fruits and Vegetables

If you enjoy eating organic fruits and vegetables then you're in luck, they're all gluten free. Fruits and vegetables are some of the most nutrient dense foods you can consume. They are very rich in vitamins, minerals and antioxidants, and they are very low in calories.

You can enjoy your organic fruits, berries, greens and vegetables found in the fresh produce section of the supermarket, your farmer's market or even from your own garden.

Among the best fruits and vegetables to consume are:

Acai, Apples, Apricot, Bananas, Blackberries, Blueberries, Cantaloupe, Cherry, Cranberries,

Figs, Grapes, Guava, Honeydew Melon, Kiwi, Lemons, Limes, Mangoes, Oranges, Papaya, Passion Fruit, Peaches, Pears, Pineapples, Plums, Raspberries, Strawberries, Tangelos, Watermelons and many others.

Acorn squash, alfalfa, algae, arrowroot, artichoke, arugula, asparagus, avocado, beans, broccoli, brussel sprouts, cauliflower, cabbage, carrots, celery, corn, cucumber, eggplant, garlic, green beans, kale, lettuce, mushrooms, okra, onions, parsley, snow peas, peppers, potatoes, sweet potatoes, pumpkins, radish, squash, turnips, watercress, among many others.

Fresh produce is the best way to ensure you are eating gluten-free, but if you must consume your produce frozen, dried, canned or jarred review the ingredient list. Most commonly they are gluten-free but I would recommend reading the labels to confirm there are no additional ingredients or the product was processed with other gluten-containing products.

Meats, Poultry, Fish and Seafood

Just like organic fruits and vegetables these are generally gluten free. This would include fresh antibiotic free cuts of beef, pork, lamb, chicken, turkey, fish and seafood.

These are mostly high in protein, iron and other important minerals as well. Beware not to include sauces, gravy or breaded meats as they tend to have gluten. Also, many chickens and turkeys include broth that may or may not contain gluten, it's best to avoid it.

Some of the best sources would be:

Alligator, shrimp, salmon, beef, buffalo, chicken, duck, venison, goat, goose, lamb, pork, rabbit, mollusks, squid, snake, turkey, quail, veal, venison, trout, sea bass, octopus, among many others.

Avoid ham, sausages, and hot dogs as they sometimes contain bread crumbs as fillers.

I would recommend checking the labels to make sure the product you're consuming contains no gluten.

Dairy and Eggs

Milk, yogurt and eggs are naturally gluten free. They are a good source of many vitamins and minerals for any athlete. You many need to be careful with the alternatives of these products such as chocolate milk, milkshakes, cheese, and certain flavors of yogurt such as cheesecake or cookies and cream.

Some of the best sources would be:

Milk, butter, casein, cheese, cream, chicken eggs, duck, eggs, quail eggs, sour cream, plain yogurt among many others.

Most fruit popsicles are gluten free, but ice creams can be a bit more complicated since they tend to add extra ingredients such as cookie dough, or Oreo cookies. If you are looking to peak your performances avoid these sugary snacks. Instead opt for frozen fruit or fresh fruit with honey.

Grains - Breads, Snacks and Pastas

With very few exceptions anything you eat in this category must be labeled as gluten free. As a rule, traditional wheat products such as breads, pastas, and baked goods are not gluten free. Read the labels carefully to make sure the product you're consuming is listed as gluten free. Luckily the availability of gluten free products is increasing, you now have multiple options in the supermarkets and stores from cereals to bread and even pastas. Using alternative ingredients such as corn, rice, quinoa and other gluten free grains these foods are now gluten free. It's possible to enjoy some of your favorite dishes using these gluten free options that taste just like the gluten originals.

Snacks can also be gluten free, there are now pretzels, cookies, and even chips that are gluten free, but us athletes try to avoid these empty calories.

Some of the best sources would be:

Cassava, rice, soy, potato, tapioca, beans, quinoa, millet, amaranth, flax, chia, yucca, nut flours, gluten free oats, among many others.

Learning How to read Labels

If you are just getting started with the gluten free diet you need to learn what terms mean gluten on the label so you may avoid these products. On many occasions the terms are clear, other times it takes some detective work to find out if a product is gluten free.

To make the detective work simpler for you below is a list of several ingredients that contain gluten:

Wheat, barley, rye, triticale, durum flour, triticum vulgare, hordeum vulgare, secale cereal, triticum spelta, farina, kamut, semolina, spelt, modified food starch, food, matzo, einkom, cake flour, couscous,wheat starch, modified wheat starch, malt syrup, malt extract, malt flavoring, malt vinegar, beer that includes malt.

I would recommend avoiding the following products unless they are labeled as gluten free.

Beer, bread, cake, pie, candy, cereal, French fries, croutons, gravy, pasta, salad dressings, sauces, seasoned snacks, vegetables in sauces, and soups.

Try it

Yes, you could just give up now and say there's no way you can do this. But if you're looking for a healthier body and lifestyle then at least try it.

Before you go on to say how hard this is going to be for you, think about all the benefits that will come from it. Nothing but good things will come from this change in your life.

Start small begin by minimizing grains, sugar and processed foods gradually and see how your body feels.

When I began I thought of how much I loved eating croissants, and cheese sandwiches, but began slowly pulling away from these foods. Pretty soon I noticed that I was no longer missing these foods and even noticed they did not sit well with me, I felt bloated and fatigued after eating them

Begin with 30 days of complete discipline. After 30 days your body will begin to adjust from fueling itself on carbs and sugar to using your stored fat for energy.

The closer you shift your diet to the Gluten free principles, the quicker you will begin to see and feel the results.

Let's get started!

Chapter 3

Nourish your body

"Because we are what we eat we can literally transform our bodies and minds by choosing an inspiring diet." M. Adams

Could eating a right meal make a difference in your performance? Of course!

Feeding your body properly is crucial to performing at a top level. Your body runs on whatever you feed it. Your meals are your fuel. If you want your body to perform at its full potential, you must keep it perfectly fine tuned.

When feeding yourself it's important to educate yourself about the meals you are eating, and how will these benefit your body. Ideally you would like to have a healthy, well rounded and complete diet. Remember these healthy habits you are instilling will carry on throughout your life. Later on you will be very proud of what you have accomplished.

Take a top athlete for example, do you think they indulge in chips and junk foods and perform better. They understand these foods will actually decrease their performance level so they avoid these foods, perhaps in a special occasion they will consume them, but they certainly do not consume junk foods as a habit.

Let's take Novak Djokovic for example a famous tennis player and currently #1 in the world. Several years ago he was a great tennis player, but faced several issues that wouldn't allow him to perform his best tennis. When playing long matches, he would often feel fatigued, sluggish, cramp up and on occasion throw up. He soon realized his issues were nutrition related.

He changed his diet completely and after only a couple of months he was in the best shape of his life and winning grand slams.

"My life changed because I had begun to eat the right foods for my body, and in the way that my body demanded… it changed my life really in a positive way and affected positively my career and my overall feeling on and off the court." Novak Djokovic.

His dedication was so clear that even after winning the Australian Open a major grand slam he craved chocolate after his win and after not eating a chocolate for 18 months he ate only one square and left the rest.

This kind of dedication is not easy to accomplish, but if you truly dream of your body and mind reaching its full potential you must sacrifice your cravings and usual habits.

- It's about making the right choices. The nutritional choices you make every day affect your health and performance. The better educated you are, the better choices you can make.

- It's about balance. You need to make time and space in your life for things that make you happier, healthier and more productive.

- It's about a healthier lifestyle. To get make the most of your body start with small steps, a steady and balanced approve on being healthy you can live with every day or at least most days. Hey, nobody is perfect.

Start today for a better tomorrow

How many times have you told yourself, "I will start eating healthier and training harder." And of course you mean well and you have every intention of following through with it, but you get derailed, one thing after another and you fall right back into your unhealthy habits.

Food has many meanings to us. For some it's a stress reducer, after a long day of work they're thinking of going home relaxing and comforting in a pint of ice cream. For others food is a way of celebrating special events or getting together with those we care about.

Make sure there are always healthy choices available to you so you can still enjoy yourself. Your true focus is in the day to day nutrition, the little things do add up and make a big difference.

Being on a diet doesn't necessarily mean you need to starve yourself, quite contrary it's all about eating, but eating all the right foods.

Good Calorie vs. Bad Calorie

So often we hear people mention calories in their food, what do they mean? A calorie is a unit of measurement of energy. Calories are Energy that fuel our bodies just like gasoline would fuel our cars. Without enough calories our heart would not beat, our brain would not function and our body could not survive.

When a certain food or beverage contains 100 calories it describes how much energy your body could get from eating or drinking it.

Not all calories are good calories. We will call the bad calories empty calories. The reason why we will call them empty is because they provide the calories, but offer no nutrients or nourishment for the body.

For example a banana is 100 calories, not only does it provide the calories but it also provides nutrients such as potassium, iron, Vitamin B6, phosphorus and more.

On the other hand we have a 100 calorie pack of chips, which is full of saturated fat, sodium, preservatives and offers no nutrients in exchange for its calories.

Although the 100 calories seem harmless as little calories equal to little weight gain and good health, it's safe to say that the amount of nutrients you consume are more important than a calorie amount.

Can we really compare 500 calories of spinach and vegetables with 500 calories in a soda with a hamburger? The nutrients provided in the spinach and vegetables will provide numerous benefits in your body and mind, while the empty calories will simply make you feel full temporarily.

Meanwhile the nutrients in the whole foods will signal your brain that you are full, the empty calories will have you soon after reaching out for more food.

RMR

On average an adult requires at least 1000 to 1500 calories to have enough energy to function. The energy would be first distributed to fuel essential organs such as the heat, brain and lungs. The minimum required number of calories is called the resting metabolic rate (RMR). And this number is unique for everyone as it depends on age, sex, weight and muscle mass.

We all have a RMR or Rest Metabolic Rate this would be the amount of calories or energy your body requires during the resting stage. This allows the body to fulfill the basic requirements the body needs to function properly. Calories are required to complete the essential body functions such as respiration, digestion, or heartbeat. Approximately 50 to 75% of an individual's daily energy requirements are credited towards the resting metabolic rate. Athletes tend to have a higher RMR because more calories are required to maintain lean body mass. To calculate the exact RMR you would need your exact height, age, weight and gender.

It's also very important to take into account the amount of hours the athlete is training.

The more hours of training, the more calories would need to be consumed.

It is a balance of nutrients that keeps athletes healthy and able to train hard for each session. Keep your future champion body healthy by choosing a variety of foods and keeping your plate colorful.

We mentioned above the more lean muscle the more calories need to be consumed calories due to faster metabolism. But we must provide our body with healthy calories, not empty calories. In the following chapter we'll go over what healthy options you should be choosing.

Chapter 4

Clean Eating

"You are what you eat- so don't be easy, fast cheap or fake." M. Allen

Think you will go far in any sport by just doing the training and ignoring what you eat? Think again!

The proper nutrition is the foundation of health and performance, and in order to achieve your full athletic potential you must tune up your diet. What you ingest will greatly affect how you look, feel and perform, yet most athletes make their nutrition secondary in their training. Your nutrition affects you in every way possible, from your skin, your thoughts, your strength and speed.

Food quality

Before we begin to focus on portions and calories let's focus on the quality of your food. I want you to think about the last time you went to the supermarket, what aisles did you visit, what did you place in your cart?

I will let you in a secret, the next time you go to the supermarket focus ninety percent of your shopping on the perimeter of the grocery store. Only venture down the aisles for a few select foods like nuts, olives or canned tuna. If you realize the healthy foods are perishable therefore they are in the perimeters of the store. Unlike the aisles which are full of processed foods with ingredients you have no idea what they are and most of time can't even pronounce.

Healthy foods are perishable. They are organic plants and foods our bodies were built to consume. If a sugary cereal has a shelf life of several years, how good can eating that be for your body? It clearly has no organic material left, or it has been coated with enough chemicals to delay the decay. We now begin to wonder what effects those chemicals have on your body and mind. Many will say there is no evidence to sustain they do no harm, yet we know they do no good either.

Organic and Natural

Organic food has become a popular term lately. Years ago organic food was available only in health stores or in farmers markets, nowadays it has become widely available in many grocery markets.

What does organic mean? The term refers to the manner in which agricultural products are grown and processed.

In the beginning of farming all foods were organic. It was as simple as placing the seed in the ground and harvesting when ready. They were all grown free of pesticides and chemical fertilizers. Foods were minimally processed, unrefined and whole.

Today with the population growing, farming has taken a turn and tried to supply more and more with the help of pesticides and chemicals. This has made our foods not only deficient in nutrients, but also full of chemicals and toxins making it difficult for us to be healthy and well balanced.

In order to qualify as organic crops and livestock must be:

Organic crops must be grown in safe soil, have no modification or be genetically modified, and must remain separate from conventional food. Farmers are not allowed to use synthetic pesticides and petroleum or sewage based fertilizers.

Organic Livestock must have outdoor availability and have access to organic feed only. They may not receive antibiotics, growth hormones or any animal-by-product.

Benefits of Eating Organic Food

- More nutrients. Several studies have shown that organically grown foods contain more nutrients than non-organic grown foods because the soil is sustained and nourished with healthy practices. The nitrogen that is found in composted soil is slowly released this way plants can grow at a normal rate, with their nutrients in balance.

- Better Taste. Many foods are now being modified to enhance their colors and achieve a more consistent shape. In return, the taste is not taken into account. Organic foods might not always be prettiest or shiniest, but they sure are the tastiest.

- Pesticide and chemical free. Research from the past few years demonstrate the negative effects of these toxins in our body such as cancer, asthma, brain function and more.

- Healthy protein. Since raised animals are not allowed antibiotics or growth hormones we can also be healthier. The use of antibiotics in meat production has created antibiotic-resistant strains of bacteria. This means that when you get sick your body will be less responsive to antibiotic treatment.

- Promote the local economy. Organic foods are quite often grown locally, visit your local market, you will probably get a better price and a fresher product.

- Organic Farming is better for the environment. These farms are sustainable, reduce pollution, conserve water and use less energy.

Cost vs. Health

This kind of grocery shopping will most likely be more expensive than you're used to. Fresh organic food costs more because it's real food. It will spoil quickly unlike processed foods which can be stored in boxes for months and still be edible somehow.

If you find buying fresh and organic to be too expensive for you can also opt for frozen meats, fruits and vegetables as an option.

Every year the EWG Environmental Working Group releases a list of 12 foods that you should always whenever available buy organic. It has been estimated individuals can decrease their exposure by 80% if they change to organic when purchasing those foods. The group analyzes which foods contain the highest pesticide residue and call those 12 the dirty dozen. Each year some foods change, but over the past couple of years these are the foods that have been on the dirty dozen consistently.

1. Strawberries
2. Grapes
3. Celery
4. Peaches
5. Spinach
6. Potatoes
7. Cherries
8. Lettuce
9. Cucumbers
10. Blueberries
11. Sweet bell Peppers
12. Nectarines

You must decide for yourself if eating this way is worth the cost. Personally I try to make cuts in other areas of my budget, but I find my health more important than anything else. Of course the bag of Cheetos is cheap and easy, but I am not willing to eat that when I have better options available.

Many of these changes might seem extreme from your current way of life. But if you want to improve your health and performance these changes are necessary.

You can choose to eat cheap and fast now and pay for it later or spend a little more on healthier food now but enjoy a better life on the long term.

Chapter 5

Macronutrients

"Anyone can work out for an hour, but to control what goes on your plate for 23 hours… now that's hard work." Anonymous

Nutrition is the most important characteristic in order to achieve your goals. Consider your body a fine-tuned Lamborghini and your muscles the engine. If you don't supply your engine with the correct fuel during a competition you won't perform half as well as your fine-tuned body could.

Even in your day to day life your body requires the correct kind of nutrition. If you know you're overweight by 10 pounds and think it's not that much try strapping on a 10 pound vest and see how well you perform with it on. Yes, those extra pounds will definitely hinder your performance.

Nutrition is different for each individual, and as such this is an overview of recommendations designed to help you as you plan your nutritional requirements for competing, training or for day to day meals.

Protein

Protein is a very important component in an athlete's diet, after all your muscles are made of protein. Protein is essential is promoting fast muscle recovery after workouts and to ensure your muscles adapt fully in response to your training, in order words, you start toning that body.

They are often called the building blocks of the body. Protein consists of a combination of structures called amino acids that combine in several ways to help create muscles, bone, tendons, skin, hair, and other tissues. Athletes need protein to assist in repairing and rebuilding muscle that was broken down during exercise. It also helps to optimize carbohydrate storage in the form of glycogen.

There are many doubts in this area, many believe that eating more protein will make you gain weight. When you train your muscles need to be replenished which is why they need protein to rebuild and restructure.

Athletes require more protein than individuals who don't train. If a sedentary person were to consume the same amount of protein an athlete consumes, then surely all the unused protein would turn into fat and weight gain would occur.

As long as you're training the protein you consume will repair your muscles and help you stay toned and healthy.

Research has proven that the timing of protein intake plays an important role. Eating high quality protein within two hours after exercising enhances muscle healing and development.
The length and intensity of the exercise is also very important when it comes to protein requirements. Power training needs a higher level of protein intake than endurance training does because power is focusing more on building muscle.

General Requirements
Research has proved the adequate intake of protein for improved athletic performance as 0.6 to 0.9 grams of protein per pound of body weight or 1.4 to 2 grams per kilogram. For example a 160 pound athlete requires 102 to 146 grams of protein per day.

As we mentioned above the intensity and purpose of training also make a difference in daily protein intake. We will review three possibilities below, endurance training, strength training and training to reduce fat.

- Endurance Training

According to the intensity of the training we could estimate that when training at a light to moderate regimen you would need 0.5 to 0.8 grams of protein per pound of body weight. When training in a high intensity regimen 0.7 to 0.9 grams per pound of body weight are recommended.

- Strength Training

It's recommended that when you are focusing on strength training in an intense regimen to consume 0.6 to 0.9 grams of protein per pound of body weight or 1.5 to 2.0 grams per kilogram of body weight. This amount is ideal to optimize muscle mass, strength and physical performance.

- Reduce Body Fat

When you are focused on reducing body fat but maintain your lean muscle mass the recommended protein intakes can be as high as 1.0 to 1.5 grams of protein per pound of body weight. These numbers can increase even more if you are restricting your calorie intake. Your goal at this time would be to maintain your lean muscles while burning off fat.

Where to find protein

Some examples of foods that contain protein are meat, poultry, fish, dairy products, eggs, soy, legumes, lentil, beans, nuts and several vegetables such as avocado, cauliflower, asparagus, broccoli and artichoke.

My top 10 recommendation for protein sources for athletes are:

Grass fed Beef

Personally this is my favorite protein source. I know it's high in fat also, but the amount of calories in grass fed beef in significantly lower than grain fed beef. Also if you're concerned about fat you can always choose a leaner beef cut, you can visibly see the fat on the beef.

Albacore Tuna

There are not many foods that can provide more protein per calorie than albacore tuna. In only 220 calories a can of white albacore tuna provides 41 grams of quality protein. Albacore tuna is also an excellent source of vitamin B12 which plays a vital role in cellular energy production. Please be mindful and choose tuna that is dolphin safe.

Eggs

I love how versatile eggs can be, from poached, quiche, boiled to scrambled eggs have so many ways to be prepared. It's very difficult to get tired of eating eggs when we have so many options. A single egg contains 17 grams of protein, and is easily digested.

Almonds

Protein is also found in plant foods such as nuts. It does not offer as much protein as animal foods, but when it comes to plant foods almonds are an excellent choice. Two ounces of dry roasted and salted almonds contains twelve grams of protein. Almonds also provide vitamin E, Fiber and much more.

Skinless Chicken Breast

If you are looking for lean protein look no further, skinless chicken breast is one of the leanest sources of protein. A single skinless chicken breast offers 28 grams of protein with only 2.5 grams of fat. Please do remember to choose organic chicken breasts.

Chocolate Milk

Quite often a favorite post-workout recovery drink, not only does it provide protein for muscle repair it also offers carbohydrates to replenish muscle glycogen and water for rehydration. If you are concerned about the amount of fat in the dairy you can always opt for low fat or skim milk.

Research has shown that when athletes drink chocolate milk they perform better in their next training than they do after drinking a sports drink.

Yogurt

Yogurt is another versatile form of protein, it can be served alone, with honey, fruit, as a dessert or breakfast. It contains two forms of milk protein whey and casein both of which are excellent sources of protein. Yogurt is also a great source of calcium which helps bone density.

Soy

Most likely the best plant source of protein. It can be found in many different ways such as tofu, edamame, soy milk, soy burgers, and soy protein based powdered drink mixes.

Organic Turkey Breast

Not a commonly found source of protein, many prepare turkey solely on holidays, but turkey is a great source of lean protein. Three ounces of turkey breast provides 24 grams of high quality protein. It's also a great source for selenium, niacin and vitamin B6.

Wild Salmon

Super charged with omega 3s you should include salmon or fish at least twice per week.

Omega 3s improves brain and heart health and fight inflammation. In addition it provides 88 grams of protein in a 12 ounce serving. Choose wild salmon over farmed salmon as it contains higher levels of omega 3s.

Whey Protein Isolate

The closest there is to a perfect protein source. Commonly found in a variety of powdered drink mixes, nutrition bars, and more. Many studies have found that intakes of whey protein accelerate post-training recovery and enhance muscle performance.

Carbohydrates

They are the most important source of energy for athletes. No matter what sport you play, carbs provide the energy that fuels muscle contractions. Once carbs are consumed, they breakdown into smaller sugars that get absorbed and used as energy. A steady supply of carbohydrate intake prevents protein from being used as energy. The body stores carbohydrates as glycogen in the muscles and liver, but its holding capacity is limited. When the fuel needs of an athlete are not met with the stored carbohydrate the consequences include fatigue, reduced ability to train hard, impaired thoughts, and a decrease in immune system function.

For these reasons, athletes should plan their carbohydrate intake around key training sessions and their day to day requirements with carbohydrates as an exercise fuel.

Your carbohydrate requirements depend on the fuel needed in your training and competition program. The exact amount is dependent on the frequency, duration and intensity of the activity. Since your activities will change every day your carbohydrate intake should fluctuate to reflect this. On days with high activity carbohydrate intake should be increased to match the increase in activity.

This increase will allow your body to maximize your activity and promote recovery between sessions.

On the other hand on low or no training days carbohydrate intake should be decreased to reflect the decrease in activity. A smart way to regulate carbohydrate intake from day to day is to schedule foods that are carbohydrate rich at meals or snacks around important activity sessions. As the intensity of the sessions increase you should increase your carbohydrate intake before, during or after exercising. This not only helps to have the proper amount of carbohydrates, but also it improves the timing so it's best suited to fuel the session.

The following numbers are a good standard to go by:

Light Training: Low intensity. 3-5 grams per kilogram of body weight.

Moderate Training: Average activity for approximately 1 hour. 5-7 grams per kilogram of body weight.

Intense Training. High intensity activity for 1-3 hours per day. 6-10 grams per kilogram of body weight.

Extreme training. Very high intensity activity for more than 4 hours per day. 8-12 grams per kilogram of body weight.

Simple and Complex Carbohydrates

Carbohydrates are both simple and complex.

Simple carbohydrates have a smaller structure with only 1 or 2 sugar molecules. Some simple carbohydrates include sucrose, sugar found in candy, soda, juice. They are the fastest source of energy, as they are quickly digested, but only last for a short period of time. They tend to have little or no vitamins and minerals.

Complex carbohydrates are made of many sugar molecules looped together like a necklace. They are commonly rich in fiber, and health promoting. Complex carbohydrates are usually found in whole plant foods and, hence, are also often full of vitamins and minerals. Examples would be cassava, yam, white potato, green vegetables, peas, sweet potatoes, pumpkin and other vegetables.

My top 5 recommendation for carbohydrate sources for athletes are:

Sweet Potatoes

One of my favorite carbohydrates since it provides so many nutrients in each bite. They are very high in antioxidants and potassium which helps sooth sore muscles. One cup equals 27 grams of carbs.

Berries

You name it, strawberries, blueberries, blackberries, and other berries are among the most nutritious sources of carbohydrates. They are not the most concentrated source of carbohydrates with only 12grams in one cup but they are extremely rich in vitamins, minerals and phytonutrients.

Bananas

The most common snack for athletes is easy to digest and loaded with fast acting carbohydrates. Bananas are a great pre or post exercise snack with 31 grams of carbohydrates.

Chestnuts

They are a great snack that provides quite a bit of fiber, vitamin C and folic acid. Chestnuts can be served roasted, in soups, stuffing and many more ways. Compared to other nuts chestnuts provide less than one gram of fat per ounce.

Oranges

They are an excellent option instead of bananas. One orange alone contains all the daily vitamin C requirements. Opt for the fruit instead of the juice so you can enjoy the benefits of the fiber as well.

Healthy Fats

Contrary to popular belief eating fat does not make you fat. It's the kind of fat you choose to eat that can make you fat.

Fat is one of the 3 macronutrients together with protein and carbohydrates that supply calories to the body. Fat provides 9 calories per gram which is more than twice the number offered by protein or carbohydrates.

Fat is actually one of the critical nutrients for optimal health and is essential for the proper functioning on the body. Fats provide essential fatty acids not made by the body and must be attained from food.

Omega-3 and Omega-6 fatty acids are required for normal growth and development and for the standard functioning of the brain and nervous system. Fat is the main storage source for the body's extra calories. It fills the fat cells that help insulate the body and it is also an important energy source. Fat is a fuel source for low-level to modest exercise such as walking or jogging, and is very important for extended endurance trials that are at lower intensities. After the body has used up all the calories from the carbohydrates consumed which normally occurs in the first 20-30 minutes of exercise it begins to rely on the calories from fat.

While fat is easily deposited in the body and is calorie-dense, it also takes longer to breakdown and digest. It can take up to 6 hours to be converted into a usable form of energy. This would clearly identify fat unsuitable as a pre- exercise snack and is why we choose carbohydrates to fuel our activities.

When consuming, choose "good fats" such as polyunsaturated and monounsaturated fats which are found in fish, nuts, seeds, canola and olive oils, flax seeds and avocados.

Do not eat foods with "bad fats" such as potato chips, pizza, ice cream or any solid fat. They contain trans fats and saturated fats. Too much of these have been linked to health problems such as obesity, high cholesterol, heart disease and poor athletic performance.

Fats should represent no more than 25% to 30% of your total calorie intake. High-fat foods must be avoided as they can cause uneasiness if eaten too close to the start of physical activity. No consumption of trans fats and saturated fats. Emphasize healthy fats that are found in avocados, tuna, canola oil, soy, and nuts.

My top 5 recommendation for fat sources for athletes are:

Salmon

Salmon is the king of the fish. Not only is it an excellent source of protein, salmon is one of the best food sources of omega 3 fats.

Flaxseed oil

We often cook with oils, and use oil in our salads and day to day meals, why not use oil that includes many of the same benefits as fish oil including a high level of Omega 3s. It's important to note that consuming flaxseeds alone we will not intake the same amount of omega 3s, flaxseeds must be ground up to release its fat content.

Avocados

Avocados are high in fat, but most of the fat in an avocado is in fact monounsaturated which is the heart-healthy kind that helps lower bad cholesterol. They make an excellent substitution for butter or cream cheese when needed.

Nuts

Walnuts, almonds, sunflower seeds, pistachios and pumpkin seeds are all very special nuts. They contain nutrients such as selenium, lutein, and are very high in vitamin E. Many of them are high in Omega 3 or Omega 6, they provide a good amount of fiber and are great for on the go snacks.

Eggs

Over the years eggs yolks have received a terrible reputation, when in fact they are full of nutrients and healthy fats. One entire egg contains 5 grams of fat but only 1.5 grams are saturated. Eggs also provide choline, one yolk can provide as much 300 micrograms of choline. This helps regulate the brain, nervous system and cardiovascular system.

Chapter 6

Micronutrients

"You are given the opportunity to nourish your body with every bite and sip you take." M. Correa

Vitamins are vital elements that must be consumed because the body does not produce them by itself. They are essential to maintain healthy and balanced body functions.

Fruits and vegetables contain vitamins, minerals and antioxidants that are essential to maintaining a healthy and balanced diet. Examples are: Oranges, a great source for vitamin c, bananas for potassium, and carrots for beta carotene.

Two important minerals to consider in athletes are Calcium and Iron. Calcium helps build stronger bones, which decreases the chance of them breaking under stress or heavy activity. You can find calcium in many dairy products, such as milk, yogurt, and cheese. Also include dark, green leafy vegetables and calcium-fortified products, like orange juice as good sources of calcium.

Now we'll go into several important vitamins and minerals and better understand how they help us and where we can find them.

Vitamin A

Well known for proper vision development, it also has many other benefits. It maintains red and white blood cell production and activity. Promotes a healthy immune system, and keep skin healthy.

An optimal daily intake for a male would be 900 micrograms and for a female would be 700 micrograms.

Good sources of Vitamin A are eggs, milk, liver and giblets, cod liver oil, squash, sweet potato, carrots, kale, apricot, peaches, cantaloupe, papaya, and mango.

In order to reach your optimal daily intake these foods contain a good amount of Vitamin A. It's important to remember that many vegetables loose many vitamins and nutrients when cooked.

Cod liver oil 1 teaspoon = 1350 mcg

Kale ½ cup = 443 mcg

Carrots ½ cup = 538 mcg

Cantaloupe ½ melon = 467 mcg

Spinach ½ cup = 573 mcg

Sweet Potato ½ cup = 961 mcg

Vitamin C

Vitamin C is essential for the biosynthesis of collagen. Collagen is the main protein used as connective tissue in the body. Collagen is especially important for healthy joints, ligaments, and bones. Other benefits of vitamin C include a boost in the immune system, supports in wound healing and improves brain function.

An optimal daily intake for a male or female would be 45 to 75 micrograms.

Good sources of Vitamin C are citrus fruits, leafy greens, peppers, and cauliflower.

In order to reach your optimal daily these foods contain a good amount of Vitamin C.

Red pepper raw ½ cup = 95 mcg

Orange juice ¾ cup = 93 mcg

Broccoli cooked ½ cup = 51 mcg

Kiwi fruit = 64 mcg

Strawberries ½ cup = 49 mcg

Vitamin D

Vitamin D is vital for proper calcium metabolism. Bone density is linked directly to this vitamin, as well as a good nervous system function and immunity.

This vitamin is a special one, it allows your body to manufacture Vitamin D when you get sunlight on your skin. No need to bask in the sunlight, no more than few minutes a day are required.

Vitamin D is not easily found in food in nature, which is why many products are now fortified with this Vitamin. Such as milk, yogurt, and fortified cereals.

An optimal daily intake for a male or female would be 15 mcg.

Good sources of Vitamin D are:

Fortified milk 1 cup = 2.4 mcg

Salmon 3 oz. = 13 mcg

Egg yolk 1 = 0.5 mcg

Vitamin E

Vitamin E is also called the excellent vitamin. It pertains to a family of eight antioxidants and as such protects our bodies from damage. Constantly battling free radicals protects essential lipids and maintains the balance of cell membranes. Naturally an anti-inflammatory, it aids in muscle wellness.

An optimal daily intake for a male or female would be15 micrograms.

Good sources of Vitamin E are nuts, seeds, avocado, wheat grains, and oils.

In order to reach your optimal daily these foods contain a good amount of Vitamin E.

Wheat germ oil 1 tablespoon = 20 mcg

Sunflower seeds 1 ounce = 7.4 mcg

Peanut butter 2 tablespoons = 2.9 mcg

Almonds roasted 1 ounce = 6.8 mcg

Vitamin K

The K in vitamin K is from German origin for "Koagulation" which means coagulation in German. This vitamin is essential for coagulation in our bodies. Deficiencies are visible with easy bruising, nosebleeds, and heavy menstrual periods.

An optimal daily intake for a male would be 80 mcg or female would be 65 micrograms.

Vitamin K is readily available in many foods we eat day to day, but is especially concentrated in leafy greens.

Kale ½ cup = 531 mcg

Spinach ½ cup = 444 mcg

Broccoli 1 cup = 220 mcg

Swiss Chard 1 cup = 290 mcg

Minerals

Minerals are nutrients your body requires to function properly. They are consumed mostly in animal and plant form. Without these minerals we would be prone to illness, and a lack of performance.

Zinc

Zinc is a trace element that is found in natural foods, fortified foods and as a dietary supplement. It aids in the breakdown of protein, fat and carbohydrates. It also assists in wound healing and immune wellbeing. Zinc deficiency is dangerous because it supports proper growth and development of the body.

An optimal daily intake for a male and female would be 8 to 11 micrograms.

Zinc is readily available in many foods we eat day to day such as seafood, chicken, fortified cereals, and beef.

Lobster 3 ounces = 3.4 mcg

Chicken 3 ounces = 2.4 mcg

Fortified cereal ¾ cup = 3.8 mcg

Potassium

This mineral and electrolyte is important enough to make our heart beat. Yes, its functions include the transmission of nervous system signals, muscle movement, and a steady heartbeat. Potassium also lowers blood pressure and also helps our bones.

This mineral is essential to any athlete any deficiency leads to muscle cramping, vomiting and fatigue.

An optimal daily intake for a male and female would be approximately 2000 mg.

Many sports drinks include potassium, and we often see athletes eating a banana or two which also contains potassium. But these foods are also good sources:

Plums ½ cup = 637 mg

Baked Potatoes = 926 mg

Raisins ½ cup = 598 mg

Banana = 422 mg

Iron

Iron is essential for growth, development, synthesis of several hormones, and normal functioning. But it's most important function is to help hemoglobin and myoglobin (components of red blood cells and muscles) bring oxygen to all the cells that require it.

This mineral is easiest absorbed through red meat and poultry. It is recommended for vegetarians to consume iron rich foods or dietary supplements.

An optimal daily intake for a male would be 8 mg. and female would be 15 mg.

The following are excellent sources of iron:

Beef cooked 6 ounces = 4.64 mg

Cooked lentils ½ cup = 3.30 mg

Spinach boiled ½ cup = 3 mg

Tofu ½ cup = 3 mg

Calcium

Calcium is probably the most talked about mineral and the most abundant mineral in our bodies. Since we are little kids we are constantly reminded to drink milk for strong bones and teeth. Most dairy products contain high amounts of calcium.

Calcium is crucial for the wellbeing of bones, teeth, and muscle contraction. A deficiency in this mineral will cause poor teeth and brittle bones.

An optimal daily intake for a male and female would be 1300 mg.

Good sources of calcium are:

Yogurt plain 8 ounces = 415 mg

Kale raw 1 cup = 100 mg

Whole Milk 8 ounces = 276 mg

Mozzarella Cheese 2 ounces = 335 mg

Magnesium

Magnesium is a mineral that collaborates with calcium to help with proper muscle contraction, energy metabolism, blood clotting, and building healthy teeth and bones.

Magnesium is widely available in plants and animal foods. An optimal daily intake for an male would be 240-400 mg or female would be 250-350 mg

Good sources of magnesium are:

Brazil nuts 1 ounce = 107 mg

Pumpkin 1 ounce = 151 mg

Banana = 44 mg

Dietary Supplements

As competitors, athletes are looking to for ways to achieve their peak performance. You can complete your daily requirements your body needs with a proper diet, however many athletes turn to supplements because they believe it's a better way to optimize their health and performance. It's important to realize there is no "super pill" that can compensate for a poor diet. In order to maintain your body healthy and at its peak a balanced diet is required. But to avoid any deficiency in vitamins and minerals a dietary supplement is recommended. Supplements are meant to do exactly what their name says, supplements your regular food intake. These are not a substitute for a healthy diet or to cure any medical conditions. We would consider them as a backup, to complete the requirements of any missing vitamins or minerals in our diet.

Some supplements will definitely help you make faster improvements in your strength and composition, but before even thinking about that focus on your diet. If what you eat is not right then no supplement can help you achieve your goals.

Some of the most recommended supplements are Glutamine, Whey Protein, Fish Oil and Creatine. From these the ideal two would be:

Creatine

You may think Creatine is only for bodybuilders or strength trainers but it's a great supplement for most athletes. Anyone who is looking to increase lean body mass, increase strength and enhance anaerobic performance can benefit from it. Created many decades ago Creatine has been widely researched and many top athletes benefit from this supplement.

Fish oil

Fish oil is my personal favorite. Remember when you were only a child and your parents insisted on you having a spoonful of fish oil every day? Well, your parents were right fish oil is great for you.

Fish oils are an excellent source of Omega 3s that offer many health benefits for athletes such as improving muscle growth, enhancing strength and physical performance, reducing inflammation, strengthening bones, and improving heart and lung functioning.

Wow, who would've guessed fish oil could be so wonderful now if only we could get it to taste just as great.

Many of these supplements are easily available in health stores pharmacies, supermarkets or vitamin stores. Always look at the ingredient list not all supplements are made the same, make sure you're choosing natural and organic when purchasing.

It's also important to keep in mind what exactly you're goals are before administering these supplements. Please be mindful and consult with your doctor before taking any supplements.

Extra tips

Include foods rich in iron in your diet, like meat, dried beans, and fortified cereals. With a decreased iron diet, energy levels in athletes decrease. Females who have their menstrual cycle lose iron every month. Another way many minerals are lost is through their sweat.

Eat more Vegetables and Fruits

Not only are they packed with vitamins, minerals and phytonutrients most fruits and vegetables also contain a great sum of fiber and water. Studies have demonstrated we have a tendency to consume a consistent amount of food each day, regardless of the amount of calories contained. Water and fiber enhance the volume of foods without increasing calories. So you would be eating the same volume of food, but now with less calories and healthier.

An easy way to increase your fruit and vegetable intake is to consider each meal a **colorful one**. Aim for at least 4 or more colors with each meal, such as: carrots (orange) 1, spinach (green) 2, tomato (red) 3, potato (white) 4, grass fed beef (brown) 5. The more colors, the more nutrients your body is acquiring.

Avoid at all times

We must have the same discipline in training as we do in our nutrition. Many of the following foods can be eaten on a rare occasion, but they should not be considered a snack or part of an everyday diet.

Foods like chips, Cheetos, sweets, cakes, cookies, carbonated sodas, fast foods, artificial colors, high fructose corn syrup, preservatives and empty calorie snacks. They will hinder performance and decrease overall good health.

Remember: **When you think you're done training, you're not done training, at least not until you've put some nutrients back into your body.**

Just as important as your workout is what you do as soon as you finish your workout. If you forget to nourish your body, you'll never get the full worth out of all the work you just put in... and what a waste that would be.

Your best performance simply won't happen if you lose focus on your body's needs for nutrients. Give your body what it needs immediately after exercising, when it's most receptive to replenishment, and it will respond wonderfully.

Chapter 7

Water

"Water is the driving force in all nature."
Leonardo Da Vinci

Most individuals stroll around in a dehydrated state. Athletes are no different and most of the times are dehydrated. Their performance is directly affected by their hydration level.

The world is made up of 75% water. Our bodies are 60 - 70 % water and our brains are approximately 80% water. I believe these numbers speak for themselves about the importance of water.

Water is the body's and world most important nutrient.

We send satellites to other planets in search of water, since we know this means life. People can live for weeks without food, but they can survive less than a week without water.

When the water in your body is decreased by only one percent, you immediately become thirsty. **Studies have shown that with only a one percent state of dehydration you will experience ten to twelve percent decrease in performance.** Now, that's a big difference!

When this decrease is elevated to five percent the body becomes hot and tired, muscle strength and endurance decreases even further. At 10 percent the person becomes delirious and has blurry vision. A decrease of 20 percent and the person dies. Yes, that's how important water is to our bodies.

To put these numbers into perspective let's see how much water different tissues in our bodies are made up of:

-Heart = 79% water

-Brain = 74% water

-Blood = 83% water

-Muscle = 75% water

-Skin = 72% water

- Bone 22% water

After seeing just how much water is in our body let's focus on the purpose it serves.

- Regulates body temperature. Our body has an inner heating and cooling system. Through a process of evaporation, sweat is released through the skin. This release lowers the body temperature to avoid overheating.

- Keeps your body moist. Water keeps your eyes moist when you blink, saliva in your mouth, lubricates your joints and spinal cord and keeps your brain functioning properly.

- Transport nutrients around the body. Water is the body's transportation service. It allows nutrients and oxygen into the cells to reach all areas of the body.

- It helps carry waste products away. Water lessens the burden of the kidneys and liver by flushing waste products away. The excretory system does not allow waste to build up in the body, as they could become toxic.

- Improves concentration and performance. Our brain is 75% water a deficiency in water can cause disorientation and a lack of focus.

On the other hand with a correct hydration level concentration and performance increase significantly.

Since our bodies lose water through sweating, digestion and breathing it's important to replenish it by drinking fluids and consuming foods that have water.

The ideal amount of water you need to drink is half your body weight in ounces, this amount doesn't even include special circumstances or training. If you're training your body will require an extra 16-20 ounces per hour of training.

This amount will increase even further depending on several conditions that may affect hydration levels. We must take into account the age, gender and weight of an athlete and how much time they exercise. Conditions such as heat and humidity will require more water. Another factor to consider will be altitude. If you are at a high altitude location you will also require further hydration. Certain medical conditions also require better hydration levels.

A good measure would be to weigh yourself before practice and afterward to see exactly how much water was lost during that period. With that number we can add to the 8 glasses normally required.

Try keeping a water bottle handy. Instead of drinking it all at once, take a sip every now and then. Before you know it you will be fully hydrated.

Sweat and minerals

When an athlete exercises, the body releases heat in the form of sweat. As the sweat evaporates from the skin it cools down the body and help level the body temperature. If you have not had enough water to drink the body will begin to overheat which leads to overheating and following to more dangerous conditions. We must also factor in the intensity of the exercise, the environment, and how fit the athlete is.

Sweat is mostly water, but it contains minerals also. One of these minerals is sodium. It is important to replace this sodium with sports drinks that are low in sugar. Snacks such as salted nuts, and pretzels can also help replenish lost sodium. Clinical evidence has recognized a relationship between muscle cramping and high sodium loss. The less sodium available to the muscle the more likely the muscle is to cramp.

Sports drinks are good during a long training session but keep in mind that these drinks have a lot of sugar and empty calories. You may consider mixing water and the sports drink to a 50-50 ratio, to dilute the amount of sugar, but still replenish sodium and other minerals lost. Avoid sugary drinks such as sodas and fruit juices that are not natural as they contain high amounts of sugar.

Water will always be the best drink for your body and it contains no calories. Drink water around the day do not wait until you're thirsty to consume water. Thirst is an indicator you are already dehydrated, and is usually delayed.

Be aware, a dehydrated athlete will have slower reaction times. Their ability to think and concentrate decreases, making for an inferior performance. An athlete who has not consumed enough water will become fatigued quicker and is more prone to injuries and muscle cramps. If dehydration becomes more severe, there is a risk of heat stroke, fainting, vomiting and seizures.

Hydration must be measured to avoid any complication such as the ones mentioned above. A simple yet effective way to measure proper hydration would be through urine. Depending on the color of your urine you can identify your hydration level. If the urine is a clear to pale yellow, you are properly hydrated, continue to hydrate at your normal pace. If the urine is a bright yellow or orange you are dehydrated, and are at health risk. You need to drink water immediately.

Hydration plan

We must consider hydrating a part of the training and competition process as such we need a hydration plan. This plan will give you a clearer understanding of what, how and when to drink.

Before an event

The night before you can already begin to increase your water consumption, as well as increase sodium and electrolytes.

Approximately two hours before, hydrate with about 16 to 20 ounces of water. The goal is to prepare the body for competition.

During an event

Every break, 4 to 6 oz. of water should be consumed. This would be 4 to 6 gulps. You must also include sports drinks, consider higher amounts if the conditions are hot or the event is of high intensity. This will help maintain energy in the muscles and body.

After an event

Immediately after begin to hydrate. On average 1-2% of the body weight is lost in sweat during an intense workout. This amount must be replenished, if you are prone to heat related cramps or sweat was excessive, you may choose to add salt to the fluids or meal to recuperate the body.

It's vital to have a hydration plan to ensure your body is healthy and able to compete.

Drinking water is important for everyone, but even more so for athletes. If you wait until you're thirsty to drink water you're already too late. Your body has already signaled your brain you're dehydrated and need to drink water soon.

Many individuals are committed to their athletic goals but often overlook the easiest ways to stay healthy and fit. Staying hydrated is essential to peak performance in any sport.

Chapter 8

Welcome the Challenge

"If you don't eat according to your goals then don't expect to reach them" Rolsey

By now we have understood the importance of proper nutrition and hydration, after all it makes up to 70% of your performance levels. Ultimately your diet can make or break you.

Success in any field does not happen by chance. It is the result of deliberate decisions, conscious efforts, and immense persistence.

Every time you embark on a journey you first imagine your destination. Next you stop and think how you will get there. The same can be said for your nutrition.

You must establish first what it is that you want, are you looking to lose some weight, gain muscle or simple perform better? Keep in mind your final destination, being the best might require a combination of these options, the answer can be one or many.

Once you have established what you want you must establish how you will achieve your goal. This is important not only in your diet, but also in life.

In order to set on the correct path you must first know where you would like to go. Set your goals high, and strive for excellence.

When you decide you're setting your goal and decide not to follow through a certain path it's very easy to get lost. You wake up one day you decide to eat one thing, the next another and all of a sudden you simply quit. You got lost along the way and never met your final destination.

Countless of the most successful individuals in the world lay their success down to knowing what they wanted and where they were going.

Well-structured goals and strategies are the single most important base in the long-term effectiveness and sustainability of your career.

Goals need to be constantly reappraised, and refocused. In tough times even injuries might appear, not always physical, they can also be emotional. You can always adapt, your path is not set in stone, even if you must make some adjustments keep moving forward.

Challenges will appear along the way, embrace them.
Make your goals fun and engaging. This will motivate you and impulse you in the correct direction.

Be **SMART** with your goal setting.

Specific- the more specific your goals are, the easier it will be to reach them.

Measureable - if you can quantify the progress, the results will be clearer. Establish your goals so you may see your progress in numbers.

Attainable - make the goals realistic. We are boosting your confidence by every goal that you reach. We need to make these goals accessible to you; they must be challenging, but still be attainable.

Relevant - the goal must help you move in the direction of larger ideals. It must make sense.

Time bound - goals have a better chance to be achieved when there is time frame in which they must be achieved.

When establishing goals we must also consider the following suggestions.

1. Few goals. Do not overwhelm yourself with goals; select a few goals at a time. Your energy and focus is designed to concentrate on a select couple to excel.

2. Flexibility. Goals are not set in stone. They may change, adapt and evolve. Physical abilities, personal circumstances, and time constraints, may sometimes require adjusting our goals. This is not giving up on the goal, but merely adapting to any new situations which are impeding you to achieve it.

3. Difficulties. There will always be road blocks along the way. But these will only make you value your achieved goals even more. When a task is challenging, more value is automatically placed on the outcome. When something is handed to you it doesn't have the same value as when you earned it.

Keep a nutrition log

Dreams are only dreams until you write them down.
Then they become goals.

Keep a journal with you so you may write down everything you eat. No cheating on this part, even if you just had half of a beer or a chunk of chocolate. For some reason when you actually write and read all these foods you can realize what is lacking or in excess in your diet. Trust me you might be shocked. I remember the first I did it I couldn't believe the lack of protein in my diet or just little water I was drinking.

Recording your activity is a great way to motivate yourself as well by being able to look back at all the goals that have already achieved.

It is very hard for anybody to memorize every milestone, achievement or setbacks in their journey towards becoming a star this is why these must be recorded in a journal.

Another benefit of keeping a training journal would be the motivation and confidence the journal provides. It provides you with focus and belief that you have worked hard to achieve your goals.

Some individuals are superstitious and after performing well in a competition they will continue to eat the same food before competing. It's in fact a very smart thing to do.

When you train or compete well go back to your journal, what did you eat and drink that day? Repeat this and see if the results are the same. Continue to experiment until you find the winning combination for you.

These journals should be written in a calm and trusting environment. Remember to be honest and real, but at the same time maintain a positive view to the future and log in improvements and rewards.

Celebrate your triumphs!

With each goal you achieved you are one step closer to your ultimate self.

Celebrate these victories!

There is no better feeling than knowing that all those sacrifices you made have paid off. I know firsthand how tough it is to not reach for that chocolate late at night or that craving you ignored for the greater good.

Your mind and body will thank you, and slowly but surely you will become your ultimate self.

Chapter 9
Determination

"The secret to change is to focus all of your energy not on fighting the old, but on building the new." Socrates

How many times have you changed or tried to change what you regularly eat? Many times most likely you've tried to eat better. You've gotten rid of those cookies in the kitchen and refused the cake at the office party. But after a couple of weeks or months your motivation begins to fade. Maybe you got tired of eating steamed vegetables, or was tempted by a late night of pizza and beer. You think to yourself, I will just do it one time, and just this once can't hurt. A few slip ups and you're totally derailed, physically and emotionally.

Commitment and motivation are crucial to your success. There are no cheat days on the way to success. It turns out that the key to a successful diet is not only what you eat or how much you exercise- it's your attitude.

A successful athlete understands you won't reach your goals immediately. Rome was not built in one day and neither will your goal be reached in one day. Be persistent, lasting results are a slow process and it's all too easy to give up before you reach your goal. With the right psychological tools your chances of success can be achieved.

Motivation

You have that drive inside you to reach your goal, no matter what obstacles you encounter, nothing will stop you.
With every step closer to your goal your motivation increases more and more, you want it bad.
People who have a passion for what they do will become better faster as they will enjoy putting in the long hours required. When they have a clear set of goals it's easier to stay focused and motivated.

To reach maximum motivation levels it is important to focus on why adversity must be faced, what are the goals and what are the benefits from overcoming this adversity?

As we mentioned in our earlier chapters the clearer and simpler the goals are the steps to reach them become easier and motivation is then evident.

Self-motivation comes from deep inside it's a desire to strive for greatness.

Commitment

Commitment is the ability to control one's desires and behavior. It is being able to turn down immediate pleasure and instant gratification in order to achieve long term meaningful goals.

Commitment is more than just the hours you put in. It is the discipline to put aside other pleasures and focus hard on your own improvement. It is about hard work and single mindedness. It is about immersion in your task, getting down to the basic of what you are trying to accomplish. It is about not accepting second best knowing in your heart, when something is not good enough and can and should be better.

No personal success or goal can be achieved without commitment. It is the most important trait to achieve athletic excellence, personal merits or any outstanding triumphs.

Past a certain point, you and only you can provide that intensity of will.

Persistence

In order to be successful you must be persistent. After setting your goals and knowing where you want to go, doing all you can to get there.

There will be days when you might feel like giving up, remember you're strong and you will succeed in the end. Keep moving forward no matter how small your steps might seem.

You cannot give up no matter how difficult it seems. When you lose hope or have a setback you have to get right back up and give it another try.

With the determination to become your ultimate-self there is nothing that can stop you.

Positivity

Do you feel at your top every day? Of course not. Do you always find it easy to be positive? No. You are human just like everyone else and you have to face challenges every day.

The difference is that positive individuals recognize that their thoughts influence their behavior and they have learned to control their thoughts. Positive people know that the mental strength to be positive can be trained.

Positivity can have a huge impact on the performance level of an athlete. Developing a positive mindset can lead to resilient athletes who continuously strive to improve.

It is important to also have a positive surrounding. Team members, friends and coaches must also have the correct mindset. It takes a very determined and mentally strong athlete to remain positive when surrounded with negativity. On the other hand if an athlete is submerged in a positive environment, they can achieve even better results.

With the correct mindset anything can be achieved.

Gratitude

"It's not happiness that brings us gratitude.
It's gratitude that brings us happiness."
Unknown

In a world where many take a lot for granted,
gratitude has been slowing eroding. They
expect the roof over their head, the clothes on
their back and coaches to be at their beck and
call at all times. Just a skip away from being
spoiled, there is still hope. No matter what the
situation is, there is always something to be
thankful for.

The more grateful you are for what you have,
the happier and at peace you will be. The
happier you are, clearly everything will be
better in relationships, work and performance.

But how can we learn to be grateful? It can't
really be something forced, otherwise there is
no true sense of it. Gratitude works like a
muscle. Take time to identify good fortune,
and feelings of thankfulness can increase.
Furthermore, those who are more thankful
gain more from their efforts.

Gratefulness should not be something that we see once a year in a holiday, but a constant day to day activity. An exercise I think is wonderful to apply to this would be to at least once a day ask yourself, what am I thankful for today?

Trust me you have a lot to be grateful for, beginning with the knowledge you are acquiring with this book and how fortunate you are to be able to stay fit and healthy.

The results will surprise you. Studies have found that after only three weeks, athletes have a better attitude towards work, are happier, improve their fitness performance and have greater life satisfaction.

Believe in yourself

An individual's beliefs are based on their personality, relationships and experiences they have had throughout their life. These have shaped the individual's character and his beliefs. Beliefs are deep inside in the inner core and because of this they are difficult to alter, but they can be changed with hard work.

The belief that elite athletes have in themselves seems so natural that it's easy to believe it's just something they were born with or it just appeared after all their success.

Believe in yourself and your abilities and you will succeed.

Chapter 10

The Right Crowd

"You are the average of the 5 people you spend the most time with." Jim Rohn

Stop and look around you, who surrounds you, who guides you and who influences you? Many will say, they are their own person and they hold no resemblance to their friends or family. When in reality your profession, your culture, your habits are in fact influenced by where you were born and those around you.

Your habits will determine the kind of person you will become. Environment optimization is important because it will have a great impact on your well-being.

If you want to be a better cyclist for example you would practice with those better than you. You could say just by being around them some of that talent will rub off on you, but replicating what they do is ideal. If they already have the winning formula why do you need to look any further?

The same holds true to anything you do in life. Want to be wealthier? Hang out with wealthy people.

Want to be happy? Hang around happy people.

Want to be healthy and fit? Hang around healthy and fit people.

It really is that simple. Have you noticed that when you hang out with someone who is very positive you begin to see the world differently, you too begin to have a more positive outlook on life.

You're trying to get ahead and improve yourself, you've taken steps to set yourself up with success. You're in great shape both physically and mentally.

Sometimes it might not be easy to get rid of bad company, maybe you have some childhood friends who aren't the best influence but they've been you're friends for a long time.

These friends are not looking out for what's best for you. When they pull you away from what you should be doing to advance just to hang out or have a beer, it can cause you to become unbalanced. If you're not achieving your personal goals, you need to find a balance, and you're friends need to be more supportive.

Some friends plain and simple don't want to see you succeed, it reminds them that they are not succeeding in their own lives. They want to keep you around them, at the same unsuccessful level as they are.

Shake them off, and start hanging out with people who you admire. Eating healthy is not an easy task, but it can be made easier with a support group.

- Become friends with the people that you wish to replicate. Go to lunch with them, see where they go for lunch, and what they eat. You might learn something new.

- You will stay motivated by surrounding yourself with these successful athletes. Soon enough you will realize you too can achieve your goals with hard work and persistence.

- Share your thoughts and information with these successful athletes. Together you can brainstorm about different diets and fitness programs. You might be surprised at how knowledgeable your peers can be.

- They will not let you quit. Successful athletes understand we all feel like quitting some days. But together you can push past these days onto better ones.

Ultimately you acquire the habits from those who surround you. What kind of habits you wish to acquire depends only on who surrounds you.

Chapter 11

Recipes

"You don't have to cook fancy or complicated masterpieces – just good food from fresh ingredients." Julia Child

These are several of my favorite recipes that I am sharing with you, feel free to adapt and expand these recipes with other gluten free foods. Be creative with your meals, mix and match foods. Think of your favorite meals and combine them into something great. Try new foods you've never tried before, you might be surprised.

Nature provides us with so much variety with textures, flavors and colors, we are extremely lucky to be able to enjoy it all.

In this chapter you will find a total of 50 recipes:10 for breakfast, 10 for lunch, 10 for dinner, 10 for snacks and 10 for dessert.

I hope you enjoy them all!

Breakfast

1. Fresh fruit salad with mint and honey dressing
(8 servings)

Ingredients

- 4 cups peeled and cubed watermelon
- 2 cups fresh strawberries
- 2 large oranges cut into cubes
- 1 cup grapes seedless cut in half
- 1 large apple cut into cubes
- 1 peach cut into cubes
- Fresh lemon juice (desired amount)
- ¼ cup fresh mint leaves
- 1 tablespoon lemon zest
- 1 tablespoon honey

Directions

Place all the fruit in a large bowl.
In a smaller bowl whisk lemon juice, mint leaves, lemon zest and honey. Drizzle as desired over the fruit and toss to coat.
Refrigerate 1 hour before serving.

2. Healthy and Delicious Banana Walnut Pancakes

(Approximately 12 servings depending on the size of the pancake)

Ingredients

- 6 large ripe bananas
- 1 tablespoon coconut oil
- 6 eggs
- 1 teaspoon coconut oil
- 2 tablespoons vanilla extract
- ½ teaspoon baking soda
- 1 teaspoon ground cinnamon
- ½ cup walnuts

Directions

Heat 1 teaspoon of coconut oil on a skillet to a medium heat. In a separate bowl mash the bananas, as they become smooth you may begin to mix in the eggs, vanilla extract, coconut oil, baking soda, and walnuts. Once the mixture is well combined you may cook in the skillet, cook until the edges are dry and bubbles form. This can take around 3-4 minutes. Flip and repeat on the other side.

Once it's cooked you may dust with some cinnamon, more nuts, or some fresh fruits such as strawberries or blueberries.

3. Strawberry and Banana Protein Shake

Serves 1-2

Ingredients

- 1 large frozen banana
- 1 cup frozen strawberries
- 1 cup almond milk
- 1 scoop vanilla protein powder
- ½ teaspoon vanilla extract
- 1 tablespoon ground chia seeds

Directions

Place all the ingredients in the blender. Blend. Enjoy!

4. Green Omelet
Serves 3-4

Ingredients
- 1 cup kale
- 1 cup spinach
- ½ cup broccoli
- ½ cup fresh mushrooms
- 8 eggs
- ½ teaspoon coconut oil

Directions

Begin by heating the skillet at medium to high heat with coconut oil.
Chop your kale, spinach, broccoli, and mushrooms into bite sized pieces. In a separate bowl open the eggs and whisk until uniform. Place the vegetables in the skillet and immediately place the eggs in the skillet. Allow to cook until eggs no longer are runny. This will take around 8 minutes. You may sprinkle some salt or pepper as desired.

5. Baked Avocado with Eggs
2 servings

Ingredients

- 1 large avocado cut in half and pitted
- 2 eggs
- 25 grams prosciutto
- 1 tablespoon basil

Directions

Preheat oven to 425 degrees Fahrenheit or 220 Celsius. Place the avocados in a baking dish making sure they are facing up.
Open one egg and place inside the avocado, repeat the process with the second avocado half.
Gently place the baking dish in the oven and allow to cook for 15 minutes.
Remove from the oven and garnish with the prosciutto and basil.

6. Green Smoothie
1-2 serving

Ingredients

- ½ cup almond milk
- ½ cup strawberries
- 1 cup packed spinach
- 1 large banana
- ½ avocado
- 3 tablespoons
- ½ cup ice (if you like it cold)

Directions

Place all ingredients in the blender. Blend.
Enjoy!

7. Almond Muffins

4 servings

Ingredients

- 1 cup blanched almond flour
- 2 large eggs
- 1 tablespoon honey
- ¼ teaspoon baking soda
- ½ teaspoon apple cider vinegar
- Optional raisins, cranberries, almond slivers

Directions

Preheat oven to 350 degrees Fahrenheit. In a bowl combine almond flour and baking soda. In a separate bowl combine the eggs, honey and vinegar. Gently mix dry ingredients into wet bowl, mixing well until combined. You may mix in your choice of almond slivers, cranberries or raisins. Place in muffin pan and bake for 15 minutes or until slightly brown around the edges.
Allow to cool for 15 minutes before serving.

8. Power Up Smoothie
1-2 servings

Ingredients
- Avocado peeled and pitted
- ½ banana fresh or frozen
- 1 peach fresh
- ½ cup kale
- 1 cup coconut milk

Directions

Place all the ingredients in the blender.
Blend. Enjoy!

9. Quick Banana Bites
Serves 1

Ingredients

- 1 large banana
- 4 tablespoons Almond butter

Directions

Peel and slice your banana into an even amount of round slices about 0.5 inches thick. Spread a desired amount of almond butter on each slice. Place together 2 slices as a sandwich.

You may place in the freezer for 10 minutes or eat right away.

10. Berries and Cream
Serves 2

Ingredients

- 2 cups fresh mixed berries
  (blackberries, strawberries, blueberries
  or raspberries)
- 1 can coconut milk
- 1 tablespoon honey

Directions

Place can of coconut milk for a minimum of
5 hours or overnight in the refrigerator.
When you open the can scoop the heavy
cream that has risen to the top of the
container. Place in a bowl and whisk until
fluffy.
Place the cream on top of the berries.
Gently drizzle the honey on top of both the
cream and berries. Feel free to add some
mint to garnish.

Lunch

1. Portuguese Clams
Serves 2-3

Ingredients

- 2 lbs. washed clams
- 1 cup fresh cilantro finely chopped
- 1 clove garlic finely chopped
- 1 tablespoon lemon
- ¼ cup coconut oil
- ½ cup white wine
- Salt as desired
- ½ cup water

Directions

Make sure you wash the clams in cold water to remove any remaining salt or sediment. Place the water, oil, wine and garlic and bring to boil in a pan. Add the clams and cilantro. Stir frequently for 5-10 minutes. The clams are ready when the shells open and the meat in tender-firm. Serve immediately.

2. Hearty Lamb Roast
Serves 3-4

Ingredients

- 1 lb. lamb stew meat cubed
- 4 tomatoes cubed
- 1 onion chopped
- 2 garlic cloves
- 2 cups mushrooms halved
- 3 carrots peels and chopped
- 2 tablespoons rosemary
- 2 cups water
- Salt and Pepper as desired

Directions

Preheat oven to 325 degrees Fahrenheit. In a large baking dish place the tomatoes, mushrooms, carrots, onions and garlic. Add the lamb, rosemary, water, and salt and pepper.

Mix well and place in the oven for about 2 hours, stirring every 30-40 minutes. When the lamb is very tender, and a light brown color it's ready to be served.

3. Grilled Rosemary Lemon Chicken
Serves 1-2

Ingredients

- 1 lb skinless, boneless chicken breast
- 2 tablespoons olive oil
- ¼ cup lemon juice
- 1 garlic clove finely chopped
- ¼ fresh rosemary minced
- Salt as desired

Directions

In a small bowl combine lemon juice, olive oil, rosemary and salt. Place chicken in baking dish. Pour marinade over chicken, cover and refrigerate anywhere from 20 minutes to 6 hours. Heat the grill and cook chicken 7-8 minutes per side or until browned and cooked in the center. Serve immediately.

4. Cod Mediterranean Delight
Serves 4-6

Ingredients

- 1 ½ lbs. cod
- ½ cup blanched almond flour
- 5 tablespoons olive oil
- 5 tablespoons grape seed oil
- 1/2 cup water
- ¼ cup lemon juice
- ¼ cup brined capers
- ¼ cup parsley chopped

Directions

Cut cod into 4 pieces. Mix together flour and salt in a separate plate. Coat each cod with the flour and salt mixture, until well covered. Heat the olive oil and only 2 tablespoons of grape seed oil in a large skillet on medium to high heat. Add the cod pieces and cook until brown, 3-4 minutes per side. Transfer to plate and cover to keep warm. Add the water, lemon juice and capers to skillet and bring to boil. Add the remaining grape seed oil and whisk together. Serve the cod on a plate and pour the sauce lightly over it and sprinkle with parsley.

5. Grass Fed Rib eye Steak Stir-fry
Serves 4-6

Ingredients

- 2 pounds grass fed rib eye steak
- ½ cup onions
- ½ cup mushrooms
- ½ cup kale
- ½ cup carrots
- 1 garlic glove finely chopped
- ½ cup tomato
- ½ cup zucchini
- ½ cup yellow squash
- 1 tablespoon grape seed oil

Directions

Cut steak into cubes. Place salt and pepper as desired. Place ½ tablespoon grape seed oil on skillet on medium to high heat. Place the steak, cook until brown. Remove from heat and place all the vegetables in the skillet with ½ tablespoon grape seed oil for 3-4 minutes. Mix the steak in with the vegetables for 1 minute on the skillet at low heat. Remove from heat and allow 5 minutes for the steak to absorb all the juices then serve.

6. Savory Eggplant and Sausage
Serves 4-6

Ingredients

- 2 large eggplants cubed
- 4 sweet potatoes cubes
- 3 shallots finely chopped
- ½ cup olive oil
- 6 Italian sausage link

Directions

Preheat oven to 400 degrees Fahrenheit. Place all the ingredients in a baking dish and mix well. Bake for 30 minutes until the sausage is cooked and the eggplant is golden. Remove from oven and serve warm.

7. Chicken Soup
Serves 3-4

Ingredients

- 6 cups water
- 4 skinless chicken thighs
- ½ onion finely chopped
- ½ cup carrots cubed
- ½ cup kale
- ½ cup broccoli
- ½ cup zucchini
- Salt as desired

Directions

Place the water in a pan and begin to boil. As soon as water boils add chicken, onions, carrots, kale, broccoli, and zucchini. Add salt as desired.

Boil for 30 minutes. Allow to cool 5 minutes before serving.

8. Wild Salmon with Fresh Spinach
Serves 4

Ingredients

- 4 wild caught salmon steaks
- 3 tablespoons olive oil
- ¼ cup lemon juice
- 1 garlic clove finely chopped
- 1 teaspoon dill finely chopped
- 3 cups fresh spinach

Directions

Heat the skillet with the olive oil on a medium to high heat. Combine the lemon juice, garlic, and dill together in a bowl. Brush this combination on the salmon steaks. Place the steaks on the skillet and cook until brown on both sides. Once the salmon is cooked add the spinach, cook no more than 1-2 minutes, until the leaves look bright green. Remove from heat and serve immediately.

9. Tuna Wrap
Serves 2

Ingredients

- 1 can albacore tuna
- 1 ripe avocado
- 1 small scallion finely chopped
- 2 large leaves of lettuce
- ½ cup raw mushrooms finely chopped

Directions

In a bowl mash the avocado until it's a creamy consistency. Add the tuna, the mushrooms and the scallions. Mix all together. In a large lettuce leaf place a scoop of the mixture and wrap. Repeat the process with the second leaf.

10.   Squash Pasta
Serves 4

Ingredients

- 4 yellow medium squash
- 1 tablespoon olive oil
- ¼ cup Pine nuts
- Salt and Pepper as desired.

Directions

Use a julienne peeler to slice the squash into noodles. Stop when you reach the seeds. Heat the olive oil in a skillet, place the squash noodles and sauté over medium heat for 3-4 minutes.

Add salt and pepper as desired. Top with pine nuts.

Dinner

1. Cauliflower Rice with Shrimp
Serves 2-3

Ingredients

- 1 large head of Cauliflower
- ½ onion finely chopped
- 1 garlic clove finely chopped
- 1 tablespoon coconut oil
- Salt and Pepper as desired
- 1 lb. Peeled and Washed Shrimp

Directions

Remove leaves and stem from cauliflower. Grate the remainder of the cauliflower head until it resembles rice.
Add coconut oil to skillet and set to medium heat. Introduce the shrimp, onion and garlic until slightly brown and shrimp is fully cooked. Add in grated cauliflower, salt and pepper and stir until heated. Serve immediately.

2. Baked Salmon with asparagus
Serves 4

Ingredients

- 4 wild salmon steaks
- 1 lemon sliced
- 1 garlic clove finely chopped
- ½ cup fresh dill
- 16 sprigs of asparagus
- Salt and Pepper as desired
- 2 tablespoons olive oil

Directions

Preheat the oven to 350 degrees Fahrenheit. In a baking sheet prepare 4 medium size aluminum foils, these should be big enough to place the salmon. Place the salmon in each foil, place salt and pepper as desired. Drizzle ½ tablespoon of olive oil on each salmon, rub with garlic and dill. Place 1 slice of lemon in each foil. Close the foil and place in the oven for 30 minutes. Remove from the oven, allow to cool 5 minutes. In a separate foil place the asparagus for 5 minutes in the oven with salt, pepper and a light drizzle of olive oil. Serve both together immediately.

3. Mashed Cauliflower
Serves 3-4

Ingredients

- 1 head of cauliflower
- ¼ cup almond milk
- ½ garlic clove finely chopped
- Salt and pepper as desired
- 4 cups water
- ¼ cups parsley

Directions

Boil the water with salt in the pot. Add the cauliflower and boil until tender. Remove the water and mash the cauliflower. Add the almond milk and garlic and mix together. Allow to simmer for 3 minutes. Top with parsley. You may serve this with steak, chicken or fish.

4. Garlic Shrimp

Serves 4-6

Ingredients

- ½ cup olive oil
- 5 garlic cloves thinly sliced
- 1 lb. raw shrimp peeled and deveined
- ½ teaspoon paprika
- ¼ tablespoon red flakes pepper (if you like it spicy)

Directions

Heat the olive oil in skillet on low to medium heat. Add garlic and sauté for 3 minutes, stirring frequently. Add the shrimp, salt and paprika. Increase the temperature to medium-high.
Cook for 4 minutes on each side. Serve warm.

5. Zucchini Bolognese

Serves 2-3

Ingredients

- 1 lb. ground beef
- 3 medium zucchini
- ½ onion chopped finely
- 3 ripe tomatoes cubed
- 5 bay leaves
- ½ tablespoon olive oil
- Salt and Pepper as desired

Directions

Use a julienne peeler to slice the zucchini into noodles. Stop when you reach the seeds. In a skillet place the olive oil and heat to medium to high. Add the onions for 2 minutes and add the ground beef. Add salt and pepper as desired. Ina separate sauce pan place the 3 tomatoes with the bay leaves to a high heat. Cook for 5 minutes. Once the ground beef is thoroughly cooked, 10-12 minutes add the tomato sauce and the zucchini. Mix all ingredients together and remove from heat. Serve immediately.

6. Chicken with Olives
Serves 3-4

Ingredients

- 3 skinless and boneless chicken breasts
- 2 tablespoons olives
- 1 cup chicken broth
- Salt as desired

Directions

Heat olive oil on skillet to medium heat. Place chicken and sauté until brown on both sides. Add the broth and olives. Allow to cook for another 7-8 minutes depending on the thickness of the chicken. Place the chicken on the serving plate. Leave the broth and olives on high heat until it thicken 3-4 minutes. Place the sauce on the chicken. Serve immediately.

7. Lettuce Turkey Burgers

Serves 4 burgers

Ingredients

- 1 lb. ground turkey
- ¼ cup onion finely chopped
- Salt and Pepper as desired
- 1 tablespoon coconut oil
- 4 Large Lettuce leaves

Directions

In a large bowl mix the turkey, salt, pepper and onions together with a fork. With this mixture form 4 patties. Heat skillet to medium-high heat and add the coconut oil. Cook the burgers until browned on both sides time depends on the term desired.

Remove from skillet and allow to cool for 5 minutes. Wrap each burger with a large lettuce leaf.

8. Double Noodle Beef
Serves 2-3

Ingredients

- 1 onion diced
- 2 cups kale or spinach finely chopped
- 1 zucchini julienne sliced
- 1 squash julienne sliced
- 1 lb. flank steak stir fry sliced
- 1 tablespoon coconut oil
- Salt as desired.

Directions

Heat skillet to medium-high heat and add coconut oil. Add the steak and onion to the skillet. Cook until brown for around 5-6 minutes. Add the spinach or kale, squash and zucchini. Stir consistently for 2-3 minutes. Serve warm.

9. NY Strip Steak
Serves 2

Ingredients

- 2 slices of strip steak 1" thick
- 1 Teaspoon Garlic minced
- Salt and pepper as desired
- 1 Tablespoon Coconut Oil
- ½ cup parsley finely chopped

Directions

Preheat broiler to high. In a separate bowl mix the salt, pepper, coconut oil, garlic and parsley. Place the steaks on a broiler pan and brush both sides of the steak with the mixture from the bowl. Broil 8 minutes for medium term, turn steaks and cook for another 5 minutes.

Remove from the oven and cover for 5 minutes. Serve with your vegetables of choice.

10. Rainbow Salad
Serves 3-4

Ingredients

- 2 cups Mixed greens (spinach, kale, lettuce)
- 1 cup broccoli
- 1 cup cauliflower
- ½ cup Purple cabbage
- ½ cup Red Bell Pepper
- ½ cup Red Apple slices
- 12 cherry tomatoes
- 1 tablespoon lemon juice
- 1 tablespoon olive oil
- ¼ cup walnuts

Directions

Chop the Cabbage and bell pepper into small sized pieces. Also cut the broccoli and cauliflower into bite sized florets. In a Salad bowl combine all the ingredients and toss with the lemon juice and olive oil. Top the salad with the apple slices and the walnuts.

Snacks

1. Sweet and Nutty Smoothie
Serves 1-2

Ingredients

- 1 cup almond milk
- ½ cup spinach
- ½ banana
- 1 cup strawberries
- 3 tablespoons almond butter

Directions

Place all ingredients into blender. Blend.
Enjoy!

2. Turkey Balls
Serves 4-6

Ingredients

- 1 lb. ground turkey
- ½ onion finely chopped
- 1 garlic clove finely chopped
- ½ cup parsley finely chopped
- ½ spinach or kale finely chopped
- Salt and Pepper as desired

Directions

Preheat oven to 350 degrees Fahrenheit. Put all the ingredients into a large mixing bowl and mix everything together. Using your hands form small balls with the mixture and place those onto a baking sheet.

Bake the turkey balls for around 20 minutes or until they are lightly browned. Allow to cool down for 5 minutes and serve.

3. Fruit Roll ups
Serves 10 strips

Ingredients

- 2 apples finely chopped
- 10 strawberries finely chopped
- 1 orange cubed
- 1 teaspoon cinnamon
- ¼ cup water
- 1 tablespoon honey

Directions

Add the water to a pot and bring to a boil. Add the fruit and reduce the heat to a simmer. Cook until the fruit is soft and the water has been reduced. Mix in the cinnamon and honey. Transfer the fruit to a blender and puree until smooth. If you need more sweetness, you may add more honey.

Preheat oven to 250 degrees Fahrenheit. Smooth the fruit mixture over a baking tray lined with baking paper. Spread evenly to cover the entire surface. Bake for 8 hours. Lt it cool completely before peeling off the fruit from the tray. You can store it in an airtight container for up to 1 week.

4. Kale Chips

Serves 2-3

Ingredients

- 4 cups of chopped kale washed and dried
- 2 tablespoons olive oil
- Salt as desired

Directions

Preheat oven to 300 degrees Fahrenheit. Toss the kale with the olive oil and salt. Spread on a baking sheet and bake for 12-15 minutes. Remove from the oven and allow to cool slightly before serving.

4. Baked Sweet Potato Chips
Serves 2-3

Ingredients

- 2 large sweet potatoes peeled and thinly sliced
- 2 tablespoons coconut oil
- 1 teaspoon rosemary
- Salt as desired

Directions

Preheat oven to 375 degrees Fahrenheit. Toss sweet potatoes with coconut oil, rosemary and salt. Spread on a baking sheet and bake for 10 minutes then flip over chips and bake for 10 more minutes.

5. Energy Bar
Serves 2-3

Ingredients

- 1 cup almonds
- 1 cup dried cranberries
- 1 cup pitted dates
- 1 tablespoon unsweetened coconut flakes
- ¼ cup small dark chocolate chips

Directions

Combine all of the ingredients in a blender or food processor. Blend until all ingredients are broken down and begin to clump together. Place the mixture on a piece of baking paper or plastic wrap. Press into an even square and chill wrapped for 1 hour. Enjoy!

6. Figs with Prosciutto
Serves 3-4

Ingredients

- 6 black figs
- 12 basil leaves
- 12 slices prosciutto
- 1 tablespoon olive oil
- 12 toothpicks

Directions

Preheat the oven to 375 degrees Fahrenheit. In a baking sheet line it with baking paper and brush with olive oil. Cut the figs in half. Place a basil leaf on the inside of each fig, then wrap with a slice of prosciutto. Secure both with a toothpick.

Bake for 10 minutes, rotating the pan at 5 minutes time. Serve warm.

7. Shrimp Ceviche
Serves 4

Ingredients

- 1 lb. uncooked shrimp peeled and deveined
- 3 tablespoon olive oil
- ½ cup Lemon juice
- 1 cup orange juice
- 1 red onion finely sliced
- 3 tomatoes cubed
- ½ cup cilantro
- Salt and Pepper as desired
- 1 organic tomato paste
- 1 cup water

Directions

Place water to boil in a pan, once it's boiling add shrimp and cook for 5 minutes. Remove from heat and cool. In a separate bowl combine olive oil, lemon juice, orange juice, red onion, tomatoes, tomato paste and water. Mix well until all ingredients are well combined. Add the shrimp. For best results refrigerate overnight before serving.

8. Simple Prosciutto Melon Slices
Serves 2

Ingredients

- 1/4 ripe melon peeled and sliced
- 50 grams prosciutto
- Balsamic vinegar if desired

Directions

Cut each prosciutto slice until they measure 1" to 2" in width and maintain the length. Wrap each slice of melon with a slice of prosciutto. If desired you may dip into balsamic vinegar for extra flavor.

9. Baked Eggs in Portobello Mushrooms
Serves 2

Ingredients

- 2 eggs
- 2 large Portobello caps
- ½ teaspoon olive oil
- 1 slice pancetta or prosciutto

Directions

Preheat oven to 375 degrees Fahrenheit. Clean the mushroom and scrape out stems and gills so it's deep enough for the egg. Rub the mushrooms with olive oil. On the inside of the mushrooms place ½ slice of prosciutto or pancetta. Place the mushrooms on the baking dish. Carefully open the egg and place inside the mushroom cap. Place in the oven for 20-30 minutes, depending on how you like your eggs. Serve immediately.

10. Banana Sushi
Serves 1-2

Ingredients

- 1 large ripe banana
- 3 tablespoons almond butter
- ½ tablespoon chopped almonds
- ½ tablespoon Chia Seeds

Directions

Peel your banana and spread the almond butter covering only 1 side of the banana. On the side covered with almond butter sprinkle chia seeds and chopped almonds, gently press them into the butter. Cut the banana in round several slices and place in the freezer for 1 hour before serving.

Dessert

1. Raw Brownie Treats
Serves 4-5

Ingredients

- 2 cups walnuts
- 1 cup pitted dates
- 1 teaspoon vanilla
- 1/3 cup unsweetened cocoa powder

Directions

Blend the walnuts in a blender or food processor until the walnuts are finely ground. Add the dates, vanilla and cocoa powder. Mix well until everything is combined. Add several drops of water to get the mixture to stick together. Transfer the mix to a separate bowl. Using your hands make small cubes. Enjoy! You may store them in the refrigerator for up to a week.

2. Chocolate Cake in a Mug
Serves 1

Ingredients

- 1 tablespoon almond flour
- 1 tablespoon unsweetened cocoa powder
- 1 tablespoon almond milk
- 1 tablespoon honey
- 1 teaspoon vanilla
- 1 egg

Directions

Combine all ingredients in a mug, mix well and microwave for 1 to 1.5 minutes. Serve with fresh berries if desired.

3. Grilled Nectarines with Coconut Cream
Serves 4

Ingredients

- 2 medium nectarines cut in half and pitted
- 1 teaspoon vanilla
- ¼ cup chopped walnuts
- 1 can coconut milk
- Cinnamon as desired

Directions

On a skillet grill nectarines on medium to high heat around 3-5 minute son each side starting with the cut side down. Use the cream from the top of the coconut milk can and whisk together with vanilla. Drizzle the cream over each nectarine. Top with cinnamon and walnuts as desired.

4. Strawberry Banana Ice cream
Serves 3-4

Ingredients

- 3 ripe bananas peeled, sliced and frozen
- 2 tablespoon honey
- ½ cup almond milk
- 3 tablespoon almond butter
- ½ cup strawberries frozen

Directions

Place all ingredients in the blender and gently blend until it reaches the desired consistency. You may serve with dark chocolate or sliced almonds.

5. Chocolate Chip Cookies
Serves 3-4

Ingredients

- 1 cup macadamias
- 1 cup dates pitted
- 1 tablespoon cacao

Directions

Preheat oven to 350 degrees Fahrenheit.
Line a baking tray with baking paper.

In a blender combine all ingredients and
mix until they begin to stick together. Using
your hands roll the mixture into small balls,
place on the baking tray and slightly flatten.
Bake for 10 minutes. Allow to cool
completely before serving.

6. Chocolate Pudding
Serves 2

Ingredients

- 1 ripe avocado
- 3 tablespoons cocoa powder
- 4 tablespoons honey
- 1 teaspoon vanilla
- 3 tablespoons almond milk

Directions

Place all the ingredients into a blender or food processor and blend until smooth and creamy. Place in a serving plate in the refrigerator for 30 minutes before eating.

7. Almond Butter Sweets
Serves 12

Ingredients

- 1 cup almond butter
- 1 tablespoon honey
- 1 tablespoon coconut oil
- 1 cup 70% dark chocolate

Directions

Place almond butter, oil and honey in a pot at low heat until melted. Place a spoonful into a mini muffin baking pan. Place the dark chocolate in pan at low heat until melted. Drizzle the dark chocolate on top of the almond butter. Place in the freezer for 30 minutes, remove from freezer and enjoy.

8. Coconut Macaroon
Serves 4

Ingredients

- ½ cup coconut oil
- ½ cup coconut butter
- 1 cup shredded coconut
- 3 tablespoons honey

Directions

Heat the coconut oil and butter in a very low heat, until they are soft. Remove from heat. Add the honey and mix well. Add the shredded coconut gradually until you get the consistency you want. Shape the macaroons into small balls or any desired shape and allow them to cool down. Enjoy!

9. Easy Chocolate Truffles
Serves 8 Truffles

Ingredients

- 4 dates, pitted and halved
- ½ teaspoon coconut oil
- 8 pecan halves
- 1/3 cup 70% dark chocolate

Directions

Melt the chocolate in a pot with the coconut oil in a very light heat. Press a pecan half into each of the date halves. Then dip the date with the pecan inside the dark chocolate. Allow to cool for 15 minutes in the freezer before serving.

10. Cocoa Mousse
Serves 4

Ingredients

- 5 tablespoons cocoa powder
- 3 tablespoons honey
- 1 teaspoon vanilla extract
- 2 chilled cans coconut milk

Directions

Scrape the cream off the top of both the cans of coconut milk. Place it in a bowl and add cocoa, vanilla and honey. Begin to mix with electric mixer at medium-high speed until peaks begin to form, around 5 minutes. Divide the mixture into serving bowls and refrigerate until ready to serve.

Printed in Great Britain
by Amazon